My Autobiography

Including Life Skills

JEAN LANCASTER

authorHOUSE

AuthorHouse™
1663 Liberty Drive
Bloomington, IN 47403
www.authorhouse.com
Phone: 833-262-8899

Published by AuthorHouse 09/10/2021

ISBN: 978-1-6655-2518-3 (sc)
ISBN: 978-1-6655-2517-6 (e)

Library of Congress Control Number: 2021909398

Print information available on the last page.

Any people depicted in stock imagery provided by Getty Images are models, and such images are being used for illustrative purposes only.
Certain stock imagery © Getty Images.

This book is printed on acid-free paper.

I dedicate this book to my ancestors and my children. My ancestors had very little in life but survived happily with what they had. My sons and daughters have better lives but should always remember their ancestors.

We were given lives to enjoy, and we are all able to adjust and make changes!

CHAPTER 1

I WAS THE SECOND OF SEVEN children, six girls and one boy. When I was born, my father was in the navy in England, and my mother couldn't cope with two small children, so my grandparents took my older sister to live with them.

Eventually, my mother gave birth to six girls one every eighteen months. Women in those days had lots of children and thus not much time for themselves.

My father retired from the navy and started working in the coal mines. He was a hard-working man and made sure he provided for his family.

In the early 1950s in England, people had to walk everywhere—to their jobs, school, and to shop. Few had cars, so they would rely on buses to get them to their destinations if they didn't walk there.

It was very cold and damp in the winter in England, and even though we had fireplaces in every room of our house, we couldn't afford coal to heat all the rooms, so we heated just the living room. The houses were not insulated well, and we had to tolerate a lot of cold. We would put extra blankets on our beds and sleep with hot water bottles. In the morning, we would wake up to cold noses and frost on the windows.

We handled our laundry by heating a gas water heater in the bathroom. Then we washed the clothes in the bathtub. It was a big job to wash all the clothes and rinse them in cold water. Then we had to hang all the laundry on clothes lines outside or inside on a clothes horse—a wooden frame—around the fireplace in the living room. That of course was when we had extra coal for the fireplace.

We had meters for the gas and electricity. Occasionally, we would run out of money and have to wait until my father got paid to have what we needed. My father had two and sometimes three jobs—interior-exterior decorating, lorry driving for my grandfather, and working part time at a pub. He was a very conscientious man and cared so much about his jobs and his family.

Family members didn't say, "I love you," but we all did love one another.

I was a very sick child; I suffered through bouts of anemia, tonsillitis, and yellow jaundice. I had to be quarantined with yellow jaundice; I was afraid that I might die. Nurses and family members had to wear masks when they were around me because it was contagious. When I was sent home from the hospital, my mother nursed me back to health.

I wrote her a letter telling her how much I loved her and that I didn't want to die. She thought I was expressing unusually deep emotions and reassured me that I wouldn't die. Families didn't really express their emotions very often; they probably were not taught that it was okay to have feelings of sadness, fear, and confusion.

I used to cry a lot when I was younger and especially when I was disciplined. But thank God, we had rules and guidance from my wonderful parents.

Some of our relatives lived on our street, and we knew many of our neighbors. Everyone was friendly and cared about one another. We could borrow a cup of sugar or a jug of milk from someone if we ran out. Oh, the good years of closeness! Where have they gone?

My mother enjoyed cooking very much and could make a banquet relying on a small amount of ingredients. With such large families, women knew how to provide very well. God bless them for that!

School was where we all learned the regular subjects including anatomy. Parents didn't discuss such topics, so it was good that we learned about them in school. When I started to menstruate, I thought I was going to bleed to death! My mother told me not to kiss any boys. We were told that storks delivered babies. How misled we were because in those days, parents did not know how to explain life's important issues. Thank God the facts of life are now taught at home and in school.

My siblings and I attended Sunday school at church, but our parents didn't go. I had so many questions at church and at home that were not answered; adults didn't always have the answers we needed, so we were left not knowing many things. I thank God for providing me with insight and understanding and the ability to keep learning.

I used to visit an African classmate's home and got to know her parents. Her mother fed me frequently, and the meals I had with them were very tasty. I also had a friend from India whose home I visited as well; I developed a taste for spicy Indian food there. It was nice having friends from other countries and learning about different cultures and customs.

We are all given lives to live, and we should accept one another as brothers and sisters; prejudice against and ignorance of other cultures should not exist.

I thank my wonderful parents and family for doing their best to provide and raise the seven of us. We were taught to respect others, and we were disciplined as necessary; we learned the requirements for becoming better people.

In general, young people's education stopped when they turned fifteen if their families could not afford college for them. My parents couldn't afford to send us to college, so we had to go to work. We turned our pay over to our parents to help with the household expenses, but we did receive pocket money to buy clothes and personal needs. What a difference now! Parents provide so much for their children. Do the children really appreciate that or continually expect more and more?

My first job was in the office of a car dealership. I learned filing, shorthand, and typing on the job. Using a manual typewriter whose keys would jam was difficult especially as I was required to increase my typing speed to sixty words a minute. I did accomplish that, but oh thank God for computers!

I had other jobs as a teenager including at a factory making bras and girdles. Girdles were to keep stockings up with suspenders and also to slim a woman's torso. The production line in the factory was nerve-racking and stressful; we had to produce if we wanted to get paid.

I also had a job at a supermarket. I spent some time in the produce department packing fruits and vegetables; the area was very cold to keep the food fresh. I also bagged groceries for customers at the cash register. Some customers were very particular wanting certain items in different bags, but we were told the customer was always right. Being pleasant and patient with customers was sometimes difficult. I had to take deep breaths while serving customers to overcome my anxiety.

As time progressed, I started dating, but I was so shy. The first man I met was eight years older. We had a brief relationship during which time I conceived a child. Being inexperienced, I was devastated and felt so embarrassed.

My parents were annoyed, but because the relationship ended, they were supportive and offered to adopt my child. I decided to become a single mother, but that was difficult. I became very depressed and felt so hurt. However, I overcame the insecurity with a lot of support from my parents and friends.

I met another man, who was married, and we became close friends. His marriage was not good, and he needed companionship to get through it all. As time went by, we had each other to love, and I conceived a son with him.

I transported my two sons in a perambulator—a baby carriage. The younger was inside and the elder was on a seat at the front of the pram.

Eventually, after many problems, my friend divorced, and we decided to immigrate to Canada. We had to marry first, so we had a register office ceremony at the city hall with two friends as witnesses.

Leaving my family and friends and England was traumatic, and I was very emotional about that. Starting a new life in a cold, harsh climate was hard, but we can always adapt and survive. We had to buy clothes appropriate for the cold Canadian winters. I had not seen so much snow in all my life, but at age twenty-seven, I was strong enough to cope.

Getting used to a new life took around two years, and during that time, I made some friends, worked as a personal support worker in a nursing home, and learned to drive. It was necessary to drive in Ontario if you did not want to wait for buses in the bitter cold.

I found Canadians to be different from the British; Canadians tended to be reluctant to talk with you if they did not know you. Nonetheless, I reached out with conversation and made friends.

Over the years, my father and other relatives came to visit. My father didn't enjoy the hot weather in Ontario during the summer, but he still had a good time. One of my sisters came during the winter and broke a heel on her fashionable boots just as I had when I first moved there. My first experience of freezing rain with those boots on was not fun. I slipped and fell on the ice, so I quickly replaced them with appropriate flat winter boots.

In time, my husband adopted my elder son, who had never met his biological father, who had married and chose not to be a part of his son's life.

I had two other children, a boy and a girl, and became mother to my husband's older daughter.

During my marriage, I came to see that my husband and I had a good relationship, but I felt that some things were missing. We did not always communicate well with each other, and I ended up feeling discouraged.

Since then, I have learned that communication, consideration, and cooperation are so important in marriage. If those things along with trust are not there, the marriage will not work.

CHAPTER 2

WHAT FOLLOWS IS NOT TAUGHT in school and really not at home either.

People need friendship; that should be number one on the list. Instead of physical or sexual attraction, which is how people usually meet, there should be a close friendship. That allows couples to see what they have in common—number two on the list. If there isn't a strong friendship and if people do not find things in common, the relationship will usually be difficult. Friendship—a desire to care about each other—will make the bonds of any relationship stronger.

We were made in God's image, which is love. If our Creator gave us love, we should love ourselves and others. We don't like to be hurt by others, so we should do everything possible not to hurt those we love especially our family and friends. There are so many kinds of love that we can experience—love with our mates, love with our friends, and love with our neighbors. I appreciate having learned this after many years of not understanding why people didn't get along and have consideration and empathy for one another.

My marriage finally ended because of distrust and our inability to solve our issues, but I'm grateful for some years of happiness and the two wonderful children we had.

I am happy to share my experiences in this book, and I hope that my readers see the need to have good relationships with everyone in their lives.

The Bible, a manual of life, includes the Ten Commandments. When we let almighty God into our hearts, we become stronger and better able to cope with life under his direction.

Jesus Christ said, "If you learn the truth, the truth will set you free." Also, we can ask God for forgiveness of our sins. If we can overcome the trials and tribulations we all face in life, we will become stronger. Doing unto others as we want them to do to us is so important.

Another subject that should be taught in school is the necessity of budgeting. The two most important topics in a relationship are budgeting and strong communication.

Good friends are so important in life; sharing love with them is so special. Not hurting each other and being considerate are the keys to happiness. Learning to enjoy similar interests is such a joy. Too many people are unhappy because of hurt, confusion, anger, and the lack of love.

Proponents of materialism are selfish; do material goods bring happiness?

My mother and father met and courted when he was in the navy. Her father didn't approve of that at first; he felt that sailors had girls in every port. However, approval was given, and the banns were put out for a wedding.

Mom and dad really were best friends; they produced seven children out of love. Their lives were a struggle, but they gave each other and the children so much consideration and kindness.

My poor mother did have a temper, but that was understandable considering she had to raise seven children. She had my brother when she was in her forties; she had had to stay at the hospital for most of that pregnancy. It was difficult for her being older than most other mothers, but my brother proved to be a blessing.

I helped my mother with many things as it was a big strain on her mother. We were all expected to assist with chores around the house. Sometimes, my sisters didn't cooperate as much as they should have, but my mother and father insisted that they help as much as they could. We learned that if everyone pitched in, we as a family lived more comfortably and the household ran more smoothly.

I love cleanliness and organization. My energy is alive and full of desire to share this. Many people including my children don't understand how I can be so energized and positive, but I always try to think optimistically. Life is full of energy everywhere, and it is to enjoy together. Listening to our light energy is wonderful, and it reflects our inner joy.

We need structure in life. Just getting through life continually being unhappy, confused, and discouraged is so sad. If we wake up to all the ways we can develop positiveness and erase all the negativity we experience, we will live better lives. My goal in life is to share this information with others.

Education is so important for leading fruitful lives, and education should include learning life skills including how to budget.

Before people start dating, they should have a good understanding of what is necessary in a relationship. When people meet for the first time, they put their best foot forward to make a good impression, but they should also look for the right things in each other when they meet. Infatuation usually leads to disappointment. How can we have a true relationship with others unless we start off as best friends? Learning about each other without conditions or requirements can lead to true friendship.

We all come from different backgrounds and were raised by

many standards. Many people are inherently good, but others can lack guidance and direction.

Men and women are so different when it comes to their emotions, requirements, and priorities. We sometimes have not been taught how to show emotion and to realize what true love is and how to express it.

God made all of us out of his abundant love. If we don't love ourselves first, how can we express unconditional love to others?

We should not judge others because God is our only judge. Keeping that in mind will help us become better people. We must have a solid foundation of love for ourselves and others and do unto others as we want them to do to us.

Knowing how to change ourselves from the inside out can help us lead more- enjoyable lives. We were given life to enjoy, so we should look for all the wonderful ways we can lead better lives and become more considerate, kind, and loving.

None of us is perfect, but we all can change.

My parents enjoyed being together because they were best friends. Their marriage wasn't perfect, but they cared greatly about each other, their children, and their relatives and neighbors.

I believe that years ago, families were closer and lived within their means, but today, it seems that too many strive just for a greater amount of worldly goods. Why does the system now teach people to get into debt when that doesn't help them lead better lives? Credit is destroying so many lives. If we don't need it, why have it?

Technology is now controlling the world to the point that people feel they cannot function without it. This has depleted family time and communication. Most people used to eat together at the dinner table, but now, families eat in different rooms and most times in front of their electronic gadgets. Parents are out at work trying to make enough to buy what they think they need, and then their children end up lacking guidance and do basically whatever they want.

Cable, the internet, iPads, X-boxes, computers, tablets, and cell phones are all priorities now. But should they be? Doing activities together can be so enjoyable! Walking, swimming, going on picnics—spending time together—are so important.

Noticing all the things God gave us to enjoy is also important. Nature is so beautiful. Paying attention to what we observe wherever we go is amazing.

I love to walk, and my favorite place is the marina by the water. It's a perfect spot to enjoy the elements and sometimes watch squirrels pop up between the rocks. Sunrise and sunsets there are inspiring.

I enjoy tai chi, yoga, walking, and going to the ocean to watch the waves. Also, I have worked out at gyms for about thirty-three years.

I was overweight, but I managed to lose sixty pounds and gain so much energy and enthusiasm. Being fit is an important part of life, and it can also build confidence.

I started studying Reiki, the universal life energy. Learning where the chakras are and practicing the hand positions are amazing! Learning how to use the energy to self-heal and heal others is inspiring.

We were given life to enjoy; we were not meant to live stressful lives.

I believe we were all given two powers—psychic powers and healing powers—but I believe that not many people use these powers.

If we portray who we really are with knowledge, wisdom, and understanding, we can become more loving, considerate, and caring. This will change the way we are, and we can share that with others.

We should also become listeners instead of always talkers.

Learning how others feel and helping them change is a wonderful experience.

I moved to Canada when I was twenty-seven and had to adjust to a different climate and make new friends. I met special people from Guyana, Trinidad, Portugal, Jamaica, Pakistan, Italy, and Croatia. Learning about their foods and how life was in their countries was very inspiring. I'm so glad that God chose so many changes and experiences for my life; they gave me growth and wisdom.

It's so much better to be flexible and open to change instead of being rigid and stagnant.

I often think of how families used to be close and always reached out to help others. We had uncles and aunts, cousins, and neighbors who lived on our street in England. We would always share and care about each other. Meals were eaten at the dining table, and that was the appropriate place to eat. Oh where did those good old days go?

Technology has now taken control of the world. There is very little family time anymore. Everyone is busy doing different activities, and they end up spending little time together. Teenagers are given so much by their parents, but then they expect more and more.

Colleges and universities promote courses, but most graduates don't get jobs in the fields they have studied. Then they have large student loans to repay, and that must be difficult to do with a minimum wage job. Many people have two or three jobs because minimum wage is not enough to live on.

Oh yes! JOB stands for "Just Over Broke."

Credit is in fashion in the system, but interest rates make it so difficult to pay those cards off. If high schools taught the importance of budgeting and good life choices, we wouldn't see so many irrational decisions that leave people in debt.

Relationships and marriages are affected by insufficient funds to make life easier. The cost of living keeps increasing, but incomes don't. The government keeps saying that it is providing more jobs, but how can families survive on low incomes?

I moved to California, where my eldest son lives, ten years ago. Living in San Diego is very expensive. There are many beaches, a zoo, and Lego Land, and this is why it's ridiculously expensive to live there. I find that as a senior age seventy-one, it's difficult to live on a pension.

Then there are all the homeless people everywhere. They have to panhandle to get money for food. A lot of them become alcoholics and take drugs. There are insufficient shelters for them to go to.

I go out once in a while with three breakfasts each consisting of a boiled egg, a piece of toast, and some fruit; I find three homeless people and give them breakfast.

Children are spoiled in comparison to when I was a child. They are given too much. Parents feel that they have to buy things for them. They have too much that they don't really need and expect continual provisions from parents. This continues into later years; their parents provide them with designer clothes, cars, and college tuition. There is a lack of appreciation from children, and they become selfish.

Most people in life have a selfish attitude and feel that they don't have to share.

If a budget was part of family functionality, there would be less spent.

Where has family time gone?

When I was growing up, with five sisters and a brother, we made our own fun with very little; we played outside and spent time together without electronics. Meal time was for eating together at the table and conversing.

We all had chores and responsibilities to help the family run smoothly. When we were given instructive and considerate guidelines to live by, we accepted them. If we felt sometimes that we could do what we wanted, surprisingly, our parents always found out. Then we were questioned and disciplined. Most parents let their children do whatever they want on electronics and really don't have family time regularly.

Do we have electronic robots now? Do we need a DS or an iPad? Do we need to be on Facebook and Messenger every day? People text while they drive and walk; they are addicted to their phones. Society seems to need electronics daily.

When children and teenagers go to school, they want to talk in the classroom. Teachers must have a lot of patience to cope with a lack of quiet and concentration from students. When I was in school, talking in the classroom wasn't allowed. The teachers expected students to focus and concentrate. If students talked, they were disciplined usually with a cane, and letters were sent home to parents, who had to sign and return them. Then the parents would discipline their children as well. God told us in the Bible, "The rod of Discipline brings a child up wise."

When I moved from Canada to California, I found the weather, particularly the winter, was much better. I stayed with my son, daughter-in-law, and grandchild until I got my own place.

My son was in the military for around twenty-one years and has been all over the world. God bless my son for his service, and I have empathy for him now. Experiencing memories of what he did and having injuries is very difficult to overcome!

He used his GI bill to study business online for three years. That is amazing, and he can use it for his career. I'm so proud of him and my younger son, who served three years in the US army.

My younger son is an entrepreneur who enjoys working for

himself. This is exciting, and he has had so much experience. He is also a singer and lyricist. His thoughts are very deep and intellectual.

My two daughters are beautiful and strong. They have learned so much, and they portray love, consideration, and kindness.

So I have two handsome and amazing sons and two beautiful daughters. They were all given love, discipline, guidance, and direction by their father and me.

I enjoy being older now and choosing what I want to do and where I want to go. My time in Canada gave me so much experience, and now I have had more experiences in California.

My jobs included being a personal support worker for thirty-two years, and I also had a janitorial business. I enjoyed providing services for seniors and clients who needed a reliable, efficient janitor.

I believe in doing good work to earn a paycheck. Honesty, consideration, and compassion are extremely important to me.

God is watching everything we do and is taking notes on our behavior. We can't fool our Creator.

After living in three countries, I feel very privileged to have so much experience and to have met so many amazing people.

CHAPTER 3

I VERY OFTEN GIVE HELP TO the homeless by sharing food, clothes, blankets, and hats in the winter. It is rewarding and inspiring to help others. God told us that if we did good, he would give us back tenfold. It is good to help others and not be selfish.

My daughter-in-law changed careers and opened a day care. I was so glad to give assistance in the preparation of the play area, and I sometimes help take care of the children.

I decided to lease a new car, my first new car, and I was an Uber driver for three and a half years. When the lease was over, it was too expensive for me to buy the car, so I returned it to the dealership.

I love to drive. It gives me the freedom to go where I need to without having to rely on public transportation. As an Uber driver, I learned to be patient with those I drove around, and I loved talking to them. Such conversation lifted the spirits of those who were having bad days.

There is no need to speed when driving. We all get where we are going eventually, so why try to get there quicker? Most people drive right behind the car in front without space to brake in case of an emergency. Why do individuals have to be like robots? Did we learn to drive like that? I like to have three car lengths in front of me for safety's sake.

Also, why don't drivers use their turn signals? Turning quickly without indicating it is so confusing for the drivers behind. Most drivers do their own thing. So ridiculous!

Thank God for cars and the convenience they represent. When I was in England, my family did not have a car, so my father had to walk to his jobs sometimes miles away, and at times, he had to walk at night. My father was a considerate, hardworking man, and he had to provide for seven children and my mother. God bless him for all he was.

We can always find time to help others no matter how our lives are going. Loving others unconditionally is such a beautiful trait to have, and doing what we should do can help build strong bonds with almighty God.

If we don't like being hurt, why would we want to hurt anyone else? Life should be enjoyed with a good conscience. No matter how difficult life becomes, we should always remain positive. This will bring more positivity and create more energy. We are all made of energy, so if we share that positively, we give back to the universe. Being grateful for what we have in life is so important! We don't always get what we want, but we always have God to strengthen us and give us what we need.

I look back on how little we had when I was growing up, but my parents always gave us what they could provide. I thank my wonderful mother and father for being strong and giving their children the requirements in life including discipline, rules, and life skills. God bless them for the great job they did.

I hope this book will instill a different viewpoint in my readers concerning life's requirements. We should love each other unconditionally and care and share with kindness. We should communicate often, spend time together, and thank God for what we have. We can always be considerate of each other. I recommend meditation to relax and do yoga to become more flexible. Enjoy life, and be kind to yourself and others. Be grateful for the life you have, and live it with appreciation and love.

We are all on a path through life that can be changed to find great fulfillment.

Forgive others for their sins and see how that brings about a better life for you and them.

We were given twelve zodiac signs and four elements. The elements are earth, water, air, and fire.

Fire signs are Aries, Leo, and Sagittarius.

Earth signs are Capricorn, Taurus, and Virgo.

Air signs are Gemini, Aquarius, and Libra.

Water signs are Pisces, Cancer, and Scorpio.

It is amazing how we can get along with others of the same element, but we can also get along with those of different elements and find deep love and satisfaction.

When we have God to guide us, it's so much easier to get along with people. I think God has a great sense of humor and gave us the twelve signs and four elements. He feels that we should study these to understand it all and get along better with each other.

It is a good idea to study astrology and discover your own sign and element. It is encouraging to learn more about yourself and others by understanding the zodiac signs. When I first looked at the description of my sign, Aquarius, it was like looking into a mirror and seeing my personality. You too can discover yours!

Knowing more about each other is a reward, and it can help us get along better. Teaching and learning are big parts of life and can be used to enlighten ourselves and others.

I think we were all given two powers to use—one is astrology, and the other is to heal with the hands. Studying astrology can help us become psychics, and healing with the hands can lead to becoming a Reiki master or masseuse. This beneficial knowledge can help yourself and others. Not many learn these things, but those who do become wiser and learn to meditate and cope with life much better. We need to absorb important experiences in life and let go of trivial things that cannot be changed.

My goal for ten years now is to have a spa and provide healing in different ways. Massage, reflexology, Reiki, holistic healing, and meditation would be included in the spa, which would offer a healing retreat for those who want to enjoy relaxing more and live better lives. Many people are too stressed out with work, family responsibilities, and problems, and they need to relax at a spa and learn to switch off from everyday situations and become reenergized.

Yoga is an amazing way of getting rid of aches and pains, stretching and opening up all the joints, and becoming more flexible especially when arthritis is a problem.

People sit too much watching TV or playing games on their phones and computers and don't exercise enough. Yoga is a solution for helping the mind and body to feel more active.

When we are young, we have so much more energy and feel so active. But as our bodies age, we start to feel less energy and become lazy. That's when our joints become stiff. Functioning easily with less pain is so much more enjoyable than the alternative. So the solution is to stay fit. Walking, swimming, tai chi, and yoga are exercises that help the body stay mobile.

I now live in a quiet and comfortable senior mobile home park. I have a two-bedroom place that I was lucky to find with some help from a friend. The residents where I live are friendly and just want to lead quiet lives.

I would like to meet a best friend to share things we have in common and enjoy being together.

The keys to having a relationship are consideration, cooperation, and communication. Also, it is extremely important not to hurt others in any way. If we are hurt by someone, it doesn't feel good. So why would we want to do that to someone we are involved with?

Friends find it easy to talk to each other. Discussing everything creates bonds of trust, honesty, and compassion. Being open with each other is very important, and caring about how each other feels is wonderful. Looking into each other's eyes and knowing how much love is felt is amazing. Touching each other with compassion and love is also special. And feeling content with knowing the love felt for each other is exceptional! Not judging each other or trying to change each other is also important.

Another problem in relationships is that couples are not always happy with each other's personalities and try to change one another. It is a good idea to write down all the likes and dislikes about each other and work on erasing the dislikes. We all can change if we want to be happier.

Men and women have different emotions and needs. A woman feels she needs to be loved and have affection. A man needs to feel he is satisfying a woman and doesn't always show emotions. We all need to be loved and feel content. Showing each other how we feel the love is so important.

Doing things together can be so rewarding. Going for walks together, doing yoga together, watching the sun rise and set together is beautiful. Going to the movies or the beach together is fun. Getting a massage together is therapeutic. If we take the time to see all the things we can do together, life will be more exciting!

Always caring, sharing, communicating, and being honest will make relationships stronger. Oh the joy of being in love! Loving others reduces our anxiety and stress and builds up our mentality with positivity.

Meditation is an amazing way to relax the mind, and it gives us energy and strength. Taking a soak in the tub with candles is therapeutic. Most people take a shower and are in a rush to do their daily routine.

Using oils and crystals is holistic and can also give energy; they rejuvenate the mind and body.

When I was growing up, I took baths once a week and washed up every day. We couldn't afford to run the water heater to take baths every day. We didn't have showers, and the bathroom was always difficult to get into with nine in the family. I love hot baths because they ease my aches and pains.

CHAPTER 4

IT IS INTERESTING TO SEE how fashion returns every few years. The styles I wore in the seventies and eighties are back in the stores—bell-bottoms, jumpsuits, platform shoes, cardigans, and rompers are again cool. It's nice to wear those same fashions forty years later.

I am a very physical person; I love to go to the gym, walk, do tai chi, and keep fit. I have exercised for thirty-three years, and I have lost over sixty pounds. You can also become and stay fit, which will give you energy and positivity, and it's much better for the heart. Exercising just twenty minutes a day is stimulating.

In comparison to when I was in my twenties, I now wear a lot of casual clothes. They are comfortable, and it's not always necessary to dress up. But once in a while, it's so nice to feel more sophisticated and dress up. Most people dress casually now; leggings, T-shirts, and jeans are what people prefer to wear nowadays.

I love to see a man in a suit; that looks so professional. And women look sophisticated in heels and beautiful dresses.

We should learn to be giving and forgiving. I have tried for my whole life to be a giving person and to help others; that brings joy to me as well as others. Helping others shows that we care. Looking at other people's situations and considering how we would feel if we were that person can show that we have a conscience, and we can assist them.

Making life easier for ourselves and others people is rewarding.

The topics I wrote about in this book are based on my experiences; it's wonderful to give advice to others so they can become more caring and giving.

If we evaluate the way we live and ask ourselves what we can change about ourselves, that can cause us to transform ourselves for the better.

When I was younger, I loved music and dancing. My sisters and I were allowed to play our music in our bedrooms, and that allowed my mother and father to enjoy their music in the living room. I liked Motown, R&B, reggae, and pop. The music in the seventies and eighties was amazing. My parents liked ballroom dancing and big-band music. They also enjoyed country music and outstanding singers like Mario Lanza, Patsy Cline, Connie Francis, and Jim Reeves. Big-band music was very fashionable in the fifties and sixties. Couples would go out to dances and enjoy getting dressed up for the occasion.

Experiencing so many years of differing fashions, music, and life was amazing. If you are feeling depressed, put on some music and dance. It will stimulate you and give you a different frame of mind.

Music can relax you if daily life is stressful, and you can also relax by taking baths, getting a massage, and exercising.

I enjoy Medwin Goodall music with the pan flute. It's amazing to hear the sounds and experience so much relaxation. If you have a special love in your life, share music with that person.

If we look into our hearts and souls and love ourselves, we can share that deep love with someone else.

I have visited Cuba, an amazing place with white sand and beautiful people. The accommodations were enjoyable; everything was included. VaraDara was the location, and I enjoyed three meals a day, dancing and shows at night, and hot tubs and drinks all around the resort.

I also went to Cabo in Mexico. My son and daughter-in-law have a time share there, and they gave me a week for two there all inclusive. I went with a girlfriend, and there were cooking facilities in the room and a tub on t surprisehe balcony, which I enjoyed particularly at sunrise. We rode horseback there and enjoyed dinner and live music one night on a boat that took us around the harbor. We also toured the Pueblo Bonita resort. We were given food and drinks, and the agents showed us all the different-sized rooms that we could buy as time shares. There was a golf course, and the resort was huge. The aroma all around the resort was lavender and vanilla. It was so relaxing. What an amazing place!

My friend who came with me on the trip purchased a suite at a great price since we negotiated with the agents.

I totally enjoyed that vacation, and I thank my son and daughter-in-law for such a wonderful gift.

I also had a vacation for a week at Cousins Cove in Jamaica. Nine of us stayed in a five-bedroom house. We had no TV or cable, so we took advantage of the pool and played games. We had an amazing Rastafarian cook for us in the evenings. It was a memorable vacation full of special love for each other and sharing time together.

Family time together is so important and necessary. We cannot bring time back, and the years go by so quickly. Many years ago, families shared much time together, but now, when everyone is so occupied with other things, they spend little time together.

When I was growing up in England, life was simple. Leisure time was spent together, and that made life safer and more enjoyable. Children played with very simple things such as skipping ropes and hula hoops. We also played rounder's—similar to baseball—and marbles and five stones. I feel it helped children learn respect and be better individuals.

Even though families didn't have a lot, they knew how to make do and be grateful!

Parents had simple rules for children, which helped them mature. My father was a very kind man, but he was also stern when necessary with his children. With seven of us to raise, he had a big responsibility, and he knew he had to do his best.

My mother was a great cook who always provided for relatives and neighbors as well as all of us. She was kind, caring, and loving, and she did an amazing job of making sure that so many were taken care of. She had a shortness of patience sometimes, which is understandable. Having a big responsibility as she did required patience, love, strategy, and organization.

Oh, the good old but special days. Where have they gone? Texting each other from different rooms at home, playing computer games, watching TV, and being constantly on our cell phones has replaced family time. We feel that we have to be a part of the system and stay up to date with it. We have become like robots that function with so many unnecessary things.

What about our inner selves? We have to discover who we really are and what are the important things. Having God to guide us every day should be our priority. Praying and thanking God for what we have will strengthen us. We can be guided to see important things that are necessary. Helping others as well as ourselves is a good thing. Not being selfish and wanting to share are good traits to have.

If we give one thing, God gives us back ten. I don't look for things in return, but I care very much about being kind, and I like helping others.

So many people don't have a lot, but they survive. Materialism should not be our priority, and knowing that we can function with only the necessities causes us a lot less stress. It is wonderful just to have life, health, somewhere to live, and food every day. We can be content with less and avoid spending unnecessarily.

Being thankful is so important in life! Sharing, caring, and being considerate are excellent qualities to have. Knowing the joy of our inner selves and being content with our actions make life easier and more enjoyable.

Communication, consideration, and cooperation are very important in life. Others will appreciate us more if we show kindness toward them.

We should not be judges or critics of others or assume we can make decisions for others.

We all have a path to choose. What path do we choose? Is a career our priority? Is family more important? Do we know what love is?

Yes, we need to work, but we can still relax and enjoy family time. This will give us time to love ourselves, family, and others.

If we love ourselves and have caring hearts, we can share that love with others. Being considerate in life is so important. Do we evaluate how others can have difficult situations and wonder how we would feel if we were in their position, or do we ignore how others feel and selfishly overlook their situations?

Functioning easily with less pain is so much more enjoyable than the alternative; the solution is staying active. Reiki is a beneficial healing process that can help us overcome negativity and stress. When we feel that a sickness we are suffering from cannot be healed, it stays that way, but if we are given a Reiki treatment, it can be changed. Medications have many side effects and can affect the body negatively. Natural healing is so much better, and it was used before medications were invented.

The medical field are now operating a big business, with surgeons, MDs, and specialists making large incomes from people's illnesses. There are so many ways to heal naturally. Eating better food and less red meat and more fruits and vegetables will help the mind and body to become stronger.

We are habitual by nature, and our diets have been handed down from our ancestors. But we have to realize that animals are now raised on feed and antibiotics that are not so good for us. Nothing is natural any more, but we can consume less of what is not good for us. Having a sensible diet, being fit, and staying positive can prolong our lives. We can obtain natural ways to heal from health food stores and not be fooled by the medical field. Being careful about what we eat and how we live can have an amazing impact on our lives.

If we also care and share with others, we will have more-successful lives.

There is no need to be selfish or inconsiderate. We are given so much to enjoy, so why not help others who don't have so much? The joy of giving can create a kinder heart, and helping others feels so good.

The weather can affect our minds and moods. If it is too cold or too humid, we become irritable and sometimes depressed. If our homes are closed up all the time with no oxygen flowing through, that can cause fatigue. I like to have my windows open. We obtain more concentration and strength from the air we breathe, and that can help us focus better and accomplish more.

Everything in the universe is energy, and there is so much to enjoy and learn.

When we exercise and take deep breaths, we strengthen our minds and bodies, so we should stay active by walking, exercising, doing yoga and tai chi, swimming, and in general being determined to stay fit. A fit mind and body are much better than an overweight and lazy body. We were given a life to live, so why not prolong that life with energy?

Consuming too many carbohydrates and sugar will make us overweight and lazy. Vegetables, fruits, grains, and beans give so much energy. Sometimes, eating fish and chicken is okay but not in large quantities. Red meat is not good regularly. We can have strong and healthy arteries by eating the right foods and drinking lots of water.

We also shouldn't get too stressed. When we have jobs we enjoy, we can do them well and get along with coworkers.

We should enjoy our friendships and strive to be happy and positive in them.

In our homes, we can create a lot of energy with chi and make sure that our furniture is arranged in the correct positions. We shouldn't clutter our homes with unnecessary things; that can inhibit the flow of energy. If we downsize, give away whatever we don't need, and clear out our closets, we will experience more chi energy.

Commercialism and advertisements make people buy what they really don't need. Spending money to keep up with trends is ridiculous. Focusing on our basic needs will free up funds for other things. There are millions of people in the world who are starving, so why do we have to spend so much? When I was younger, my siblings and I wore hand-me-downs, and we patched holes in our shoes with cardboard until my parents could buy us new shoes.

I feel that we are ruled by the planets and signs and that if we tap into our energy, we can enjoy life more. We are all energy, and if we take the time to get to know ourselves better, we can become more confident and make better choices.

We all have the power to heal ourselves and others. We don't have to simply accept our sicknesses and resort to medications that cause side effects. There are many courses that can be studied, and we can benefit by living healthier lives. I am studying Chikara-Reiki-Do, which is an online course designed by Judith Conroy. It is an amazing course that teaches how to become a Reiki master and to know how to initiate others as Reiki masters. Giving and receiving energy is an awesome way to be a healer.

This also can evolve into having a Reiki business.

CHAPTER 5

W HEN I WAS YOUNG, I found it difficult to be five-eleven and to have to wear size-twelve shoes. I was embarrassed about my height. I wondered why I was so much taller than my friends and even my father.

Shopping for shoes with large feet was so difficult. Most shoes were made in smaller sizes, and I would cry when I couldn't find shoes to fit.

My grandfather was six-three and weighted close to three hundred pounds, so I think that my genes came from him.

Since then, I have accepted my height. I realize that we have to be how we were created and be thankful and grateful for what we are. Our heights and weights are not priorities anyway; our personalities are the most important things.

Looking in the mirror every day to see how we look is okay, but we also need to look at how we can change. Do we care only about ourselves, or do we make an effort to care about others? Doing unto others as we want them to do to us is essential.

As we help ourselves in life, we can help others and find great joy in doing so. We must forgive others who trouble us just as God forgives us for troubling him.

We shouldn't keep purposely doing bad things; we should try to be good. It's only logical to forgive others who do bad things to us.

If we portray kindness and consideration, others will see that we are not affected by what they do to us.

Helping individuals to see that they can also change and become kinder is setting a good example. We can turn anger into happiness and overlook negativity. Overlooking negative thoughts will put us in a better frame of mind.

We should be energized and consistent with our responsibilities and have a good and active frame of mind. Going to bed with anger is not a good thing. We sleep better if we take deep breaths, close our eyes, and relax. It is always good to be positive when we go to sleep. If we relax before we sleep, we also dream less.

Dreams usually come from restlessness and stress. Meditation is so beneficial; it helps calm the body and mind.

Being a part of others' lives even for a short time can be an amazing experience. Sometimes, people we meet may have been in one of our past lives or were put into our present lives so that we can help them or learn from them.

Life is a learning process, and we can benefit from that in many ways. We are given a life to live well to try to learn as much as possible and share our energy with others. Being a true friend is important even if we don't always get true friendship in return.

Some people we meet will portray themselves as genuine, but in time, they will show their basic dishonesty; they are evaluating what they can gain from us. This is unfair, so we don't have to continue such friendships. We can choose who we want to be and not be fooled by others.

Having a sound mind, body, and outlook on life is important, and this brings positiveness. Almighty God gives us insight to know when people are not genuine, and he protects us with redirection.

There are many disappointments in life, but they can make us stronger. Being angry at those who disappoint us is not a solution.

There are five principles in studying Reiki.

1. Just for today, I will let go of anger.
2. Just for today, I will let go of worry.
3. Today, I will count my many blessings.
4. Today, I will do my work honestly.
5. Today, I will be kind to every living thing.

It's difficult to overlook what people do to us, but Jesus forgave the Jews who persecuted him and put him to death. We must forgive others as well.

Life is a path that we choose, and along the way, we sometimes lose. The solution is to evaluate how we can become wiser.

When we tap into our physic powers, we can see very clearly when people are not being genuine. We can help others realize that they are fooling themselves by acting very poorly and that karma will come back to them when they are not prepared for it.

Oh thank God for the insight to see when others are trying to fool me!

We can all look at the description of our signs and elements and become wiser knowing from the strengths that we have how to use them successfully.

I am an Aquarian and thus am independent, intellectual, and intense. I am a humanitarian; I like to help others. My element is air, and I am more compatible with Libras and Gemini's, who are of the same element.

Astrology is amazing; it can enlighten us and make us understand how we can use that energy to have more-successful lives.

I am so grateful to almighty God for enlightening me and making me understand my personality and path in life. It took me many years of searching to understand my path, and it feels amazing and gives me contentment now.

If we learn to be more appreciative, we can put that knowledge into caring and sharing and leading better lives.

The system for education teaches basic subjects such as math, English, science, and history, but it doesn't teach life skills. It is good for students to work and realize the cost of living and learn life skills including how to budget their money and what good relationships require. I learned all these things later in life and feel so happy to share them in this book. If you look inside yourself, you'll be amazed at what you can find. Creativity, poetry, art, and many other things are wonderful to discover and indulge in.

Life is for doing as much as possible, and getting to know what we enjoy is wonderful enlightenment. God gave us so much to learn, and using our time productively is a great way to enjoy life more. Leisure time and family time are so important also. In between the learning and doing, we can enjoy nature, travel, and discovering so much. When we share family time, we should be happy and communicate with positivity. This will avoid negativity.

When we were young, my sisters and I had silly differences. I have learned that competing to see who can win an argument or trying to prove who is right or wrong is so unnecessary. I am so grateful for all I have learned, and I'm constantly learning how to become a better person and to care about others.

If we look inside ourselves, we can find gratefulness, caring, consideration, and love. These qualities are so much better than being selfish, inconsiderate, and unkind. We have only one life, so making an effort to live it the best way possible is a joy.

CHAPTER 6

A VERY DIFFICULT PART OF MY life was going through perimenopause and menopause. Women experience so many changes starting from puberty, going into menstruation, and experiencing PMS (postmenstrual syndrome).

It is so stressful when females have the week before menstruation, the week of menstruation, and the week of getting back to normal. So females have only one week of every month when they are not going through changes.

Menopause causes irritability, frustration, and mood changes that are so difficult to overcome. We are emotional and short tempered and find it hard to cope.

Children, husbands, and boyfriends cannot understand the drastic changes a woman experiences and should be taught about them and how to be sympathetic, give support, and be more compassionate.

As a woman ages and produces less estrogen, she goes through perimenopause accompanied by hot flashes and heart palpitations. It is a very traumatic experience, but there are natural sources to balance the hormones. Black cohosh, evening primrose oil, and many more natural herbs can balance the hormonal changes.

Many publications explain the hormone changes and the solutions to them. Women will benefit from learning about the solutions to this. Families function better when everyone is aware of the symptoms, solutions, and changes women experience. Men also go through menopause, so it's good for them to become aware of that too.

Irritability, eating more, and moodiness are some of the symptoms. Depression, fatigue, and imbalance can cause a man to feel inadequate. Gaining weight and having less energy are among the symptoms. Feeling emotional and having less libido cause men to suffer from low self-esteem.

Men like to feel balanced, and they find it difficult to go through physical changes. But there are publications that explain the changes and the natural solutions that can balance the hormones. No need to go through unnecessary changes when there are solutions.

Reading publications and becoming wiser will help tremendously. Everyone can become educated with the changes that we all go through as we age and have more empathy for each other. Thank God for all those who teach and write about the cycle of changes.

My poor mother and father had no idea of what was happening as they aged, and they suffered in silence with no solutions. Many people became insane due to menopause and were committed to mental asylums. How devastating is that?

Thank God for the knowledge we have now. Life is full of learning, and we can google just about anything now.

Halloween, Easter, and Christmas have become so commercialized; people are encouraged to buy things they don't need and can't afford. That leads to burdensome debt they have difficulty paying off.

Why don't people speak up to the government and stress the need to make the minimum wage higher and the cost of living more balanced? Manufacturers benefit from all that they sell, but their customers do not. Everyone just accepts whatever is happening, and people are afraid to object to how the leaders are lying and lording it over the people. Almighty God is watching how people suffer and kill each other and the pollution we are causing.

What has the world become?

If we reduce the amount of time we spend on electronics, socialize with each other, and become more physical to strengthen our minds and bodies, we will live healthier and longer lives.

I spend very little time on electronics, and I enjoy a variety of crafts and sharing the finished projects with others.

We have to work even as we become seniors because the cost of living keeps increasing while our incomes don't.

When I was young, I used to help my grandmother take care of my two aunts. One aunt had epilepsy all her life while the other was a cripple with one leg shorter than the other; she used crutches all her life. I think that was how I became a nurse with seniors and did that for thirty-two years. I enjoyed taking care of seniors and helping them to be comfortable, fed, showered, and happy.

Most seniors now are put in nursing homes because their families don't have time to take care of them. Giving care to others has been a big part of my life, and I feel joy and satisfaction in assisting others in many ways.

We can all help others in many ways and help them become happier. God says that if we give one thing, he will give us back tenfold. Rewards come from caring about others and showing kindness and love. Being happy, active, sociable, and generous can help us become better individuals.

Jesus Christ gave to so many when he was on the earth, and we can also give to others. Prayer is an uplifting way to communicate with almighty God and give thanks for our lives and all we have. No matter how little we have or how we sometimes struggle, we must appreciate everything.

God always listens to our prayers, and we can receive his guidance to make decisions and have more direction in life.

I have been overjoyed to write this book and explain a little of my biography showing the changes in my life.

Many of my suggestions can also make terrific changes in your life.

Read, learn, care, and share and you will have a fulfilling and joyful life.

God bless you all, and may you find peace within and joy in your life!

Printed in the United States
by Baker & Taylor Publisher Services